North of Paradise

North of Paradise

Poems by

Rimas Uzgiris

Cover Art: © Monika Furmana, 2018, *The Physical Impossibility of Love in the Mind of the Living Family* (detail)

Cover Design: Shay Culligan

ISBN: 978-1-949229-91-2

Kelsay Books Inc.

kelsaybooks.com
502 S 1040 E, A119
American Fork, Utah 84003

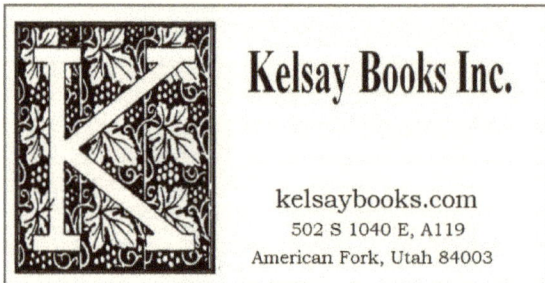

This book is dedicated to my grandparents
and their children
who were born on the other side
and who made my return journey possible

Acknowledgements

The Adirondack Review: "The Ruins of Troy", "Dark Energy", "Café de Paris, Vilnius", "Homeland", "What They're Up To"

Alaska Quarterly Review: "AfterBirth"

Atlanta Review: "Storm"

Barrow Street: "Invocation"

The Drunken Boat: "Missive"

Druskininkai Poetic Fall 2012 (Anthology): "The Jacket", "What Comes of It", "Downtown Wednesday Night", "AA 956"

The Four Quarters Magazine: "One"

Fredericksburg Literary & Art Review: "Even Death", "Postcard from Crimea (1975)", "Covenant"

Gobshite Quarterly: "We Were Dancing"

Hudson Review: "Centerville River"

Hunger Mountain: "Vacancy"

Inter|rupture: "Archaic Fragment, K.34"

JAMA: "The Test"

Kin: "No Shield of Achilles"

The Literary Bohemian: "Between the Lines"

Lituanus: "Four Scenes of Kaunas", "Return to Sender", "Shards of One World"

Litvak: An Anthology: "Something About Vilnius", "The Return", "Exiled Home", "Windward", "Exile Still Becoming"

The Manhattanville Review: "Apples and Oranges", "There is this life"

Matter: "White News"

Mayday Magazine: "Acropolis"

Measure: "North of Paradise"

Per Contra: "Four Dimensions and a Handful of Dust"

The Poetry Porch: "Catholic Education"

Poetry Review (UK): "Reflections from Brussels"

Prime Number Magazine: "Still Life with Women, Artists, and Platonic Forms", "A Potato on a Mine"

Quiddity International Journal of Literature: "East River Blues",
    "The Teapot"
Raintown Review: "Hard Winter"
riverbabble: "Dating/Divorcing"
Sheepshead Review: "Mind the Gap", "While i was taking her out
    to dinner"
Vilnius Review: "New Worlds", "Sand Piled High", "Under
    Vilnius", "Eppur Si Muove", "Snow melt on the
    eaves…", "Stones"
The Worcester Review: "We"

A number of poems have been published in Lithuanian translation
in the following periodicals and anthologies: *Druskininkai Poetinis
Ruduo Almanachas 2012, Literatūra ir menas, Metai, Nemunas,
Poezijos Pavasaris Almanachas 2016, 2017* (a best of the press
anthology), *Siaurės atėnai*

Contents

II. Present Continuous

"That poor foreign boy…"

—My 10th grade Honors English teacher, speaking of me to my friends, who thought it was hilarious, given that I was born and raised in the States. I wasn't sure what to think about it, and I'm still not sure…

North? What searcher has ever been directed *north?* What you're supposed to be looking for lies south—those dusky natives, right? For danger and enterprise they send you west, for visions, east. But what's north?

—Thomas Pynchon, *Gravity's Rainbow*

That everywhere on the horizon of his sigh
Is now, as always, only waiting to be told
To be his father's house and speak his mother tongue.

—W. H. Auden, "The Traveller",
from the cycle "The Quest"

Between the Lines

There was no map
for the trip my parents took.
Soldiers crossed the continent
with flags, changing
all the names. You can't
step into the same river twice.
And yet, Heraclitus, I stepped
into that river all the same.

From the airplane: endless pines,
fields of rape and rye. Firs
like elders with green beards.
I could barely draw breath, the air
was so full of meaning,
the language hardly known.
My mother's uncle met me
in a run-down Soviet car.

He drove us to where the Neris
flows into the Nemunas, talking
all the way, his words rolling
over me like a rill splashing
off the rocks of my ignorance.
We passed a horse-drawn carriage
full of hay. On TV, three women
in peasant garb sang a dirge.

My father was born on the Neris
near where I now live. I don't know
where I now live: Vilnius. Vilna. Wilno.
People ran like water. In the lecture hall
where I teach, our colleague
screened a map of North America

and all I could see was the Mohawk
meeting the Hudson and my youth.

I could barely draw breath, the air
was so full of meaning. This
was my home. There. Here. Now.
Then. Like a hermit crab in the sea,
or carried like a louse, Odysseus
with no Ithaca, I live in between
the lines. Maps cannot contain me.
Son of refugees. English is my house.

I. Past Imperfective

Four Dimensions and a Handful of Dust

Ontogeny recapitulates phylogeny.
 —E. Haeckel

How many years did I spend not looking
at white birches (now late in winter sun)
outside this window of my upbringing?

The trees were there to miss whenever
I mowed the lawn, or played ball,
and left home—while they grew, slowly,
mindlessly, to present perfection.

A spinning globe on the desk maps out
the motley adventures of my evolution...
But where I haven't been is vaster—

What I haven't done, what I haven't seen,
whom I haven't loved—all nots knotted
into a four-dimensional self as tightly
as what happened—the real and the anti-real

growing to perfection, or completion,
and finally, a blank page:
                                  white as birches

The Ruins of Troy

—outside Troy, NY

On the butcher shop door
hangs a picture of a
child gone missing: me—
my life is over, it seems

I am led to a great mall
where passing escalators
speak the same lines
of gates at cross purposes

and my childhood photos
on the wall of the now
non-existent house hide
in Troy like Helen

preserved by mythical time—
adolescent Achilles claims
his watch is broken, Hector alive.
And the trees are busy with snow.

Return to Sender: A Wandering Sestina

In Niskayuna, once, the earth was soft to me,
green. Trees loomed like cathedrals, tall as sky.
Churches were shopping malls, and the fox's land
grew—developed—dwellings at the clogged road.
Dreaming Fenimore, the deerslayer, Uncas, I ran
along the Mohawk. The forests were open, home.

My mother's parents, after doing time on the hard road
through factories and war, finally found a quiet home
in Centerville. In the fresh sea-breeze, under a fresco sky,
molding sand into flowers, they found peace on alien land.
There, baiting fishhooks, slashing the Sound, I ran
summers ragged, unaware of what they whispered me.

Unfilled by other joys, by love, from all this I ran
to La Jolla's cliffs and crescent bay. Its azure sky
warmed all the same each day. Here I found a home
in the shadow of Hollywood dream factories. But for me,
the magic wore out like cheap shoes in the land
of Oz. Like a hippie after the Dead, I hit the road.

In Kaunas, rooted as an oak to where two rivers ran
to the point of a pagan spear, in a weathered land
polluted with history, I found my ancestral home.
There, vodka flowed like autumn rain from a slushy sky,
and Time closed down both ends of the cobble-stoned road
where broken churches renamed a world unknown to me.

Without another plan, I took the staid academic road.
I tried, by thinking, to discover what belonged to me.
Madison was a gridded library, a white-roomed home
in the mind that never felt permanent. Rootless, it ran
precariously along two shores, bludgeoned by a sky
that opened up without limit, flat and dull as the land.

By Brooklyn's Lullwater, a heron fished from land
next to a black man, next to an Asian, next to me.
Prospect Park was a haven for my ship—a second home
in the maelstrom of concrete, flesh, and dreams that ran
like whiskey down an alcoholic's throat. Every road
could lead anywhere. So I left verses for the sky.

Like a languid hypnotized snake, the unrepeated road
unwinds itself in passing, back and away from me
and on through the places that some will call home.

East River Blues

for Spalding Gray (1941-2004)

After the tide spun me from Gowanus
into the broad, fast flow of the river,
I came to Brooklyn Bridge, coated in oil,
salt, and plastic bags like flags from
the country that lost. Above my swollen
head, stone arches soared. I lingered
in their shadow as a heavy barge plowed
the current, followed by a tourist ferry
barking electric words. Trapped in eddies,
I watched the city lights bloom—my stars.
Each fluorescence, like tinsel over a void,
flickered as coldly and distantly as heaven.

Who was it who took me to that museum?—
O'Keefe painted the arches of Brooklyn Bridge
like cathedral windows,
and the shimmering lattice of metal cables
became stained glass
illuminated by the sun.

Through those windows now, cars and trucks
bump and grind, belching heavy breath,
or honking like migrating geese.
But no gulls circle on the drafts above.
Pigeons prefer their solid asphalt
gleaning grounds.
                    Who was I ever
in all this noise, light, and cast off
debris?
            Around and around we go—
the bags, a Coke bottle, and me—caught
at the foot of the tower, our limbo.

Surely the wake of some passing ship
will dislodge my orbit. Or stronger yet,
the tide will swing. I will float free,
and maybe, in the coming dawn,
they will find me still recognizable,
and be able to tell my mother that I'm dead.

The Jacket

The leather jacket hangs
between worsted wool
and nylon sheen.

Its faded, dun hide
has been stained and chafed
by memory.

A bluebird day in Athens.
White buildings. A distant
shimmering sea. Narrow

market streets. The balding
salesman tells us it's from Germany,
and proves its worth with fire.

And yet the hide fears water.
Fickle jacket. Tough and
sensitive. A woman's man.

My ex-wife bought it.
A curvy Lithuanian doctor
with ebullient charm.

Months later, after her absence
had grown roots, rain covered
Queens again. My career drowned.

A blunt Russian colleague,
my fellow smoker, philosopher,
asked if the jacket is all right.

It's alright, I said. Just
the ashes of cigarettes,
and always the rain.

Dating/Divorcing

The West Village labyrinth sucked
him in coldly like dark mother death.
Windows were eyes that looked
just one way, and the wrinkled leaf
of an oak was a twisted tongue.

I'm not ready,
yet, she said.
I understand, he said.

He wandered like a shadow
through the wind, a night-flâneur
on winding winter streets where
drunk men spit guttural stones.
He drifted at a loss, then found
the sound of clicking heels.
Taxis buzzed by like flies.

Waiting for papers—
it's a hard time, she said.
I know, he said.

A brownstone's windows opened
onto white ceilings, warmth,
an oil painting, and bookshelves.
He froze in the memory
of fireplaces, family,
and home. Wind kicked him
with spurs. He hurried after
the light of advertisements.

Could you just hang around
as a friend? she said.
Sure, he said.

Hollywood glitz marked subway stairs.
Down in the pit—riotous rats, two young
women sunk into iPods, a man sunk into
a bench, an old-timer raving about albinos.
Others stared into the tunnel, hoping.

While i was taking her out to dinner

platonic forms were falling from the windows of skyscrapers
like confetti—
will someone please give me some spaghetti?
that's what i thought while i waited for the waiter
to arrive: he was young, false, and slow,
and the forms continued to fall outside the window
like snow—
reminding me again of how the anti-realist metaphysics of derrida and co.
doesn't get you very far when you're hungry,
and although, it's true, you can't eat a platonic form,
at least you know what you're looking for(mm?).
and since willful de(con)struction of what really and truly is makes me
    angry,
i gripped my fork tightly and made fun of my date—
a dumb move because platonically and otherwise she didn't deserve
    the hate.

Still Life with Women, Artists, and Platonic Forms

—at the "Gallery Girls" drawing event,
NY Armory Show, 2010

The sculpted pose of quickly drawn bodies,
under blue light yellowed skin, sings youth
and aging death, while the cabaret DJ pulses
a waltzing Weimar dissolution across
our couch of eyes.
                            Artists flick their chalk,
pencils, pens—coaxing dim tools
to caress white paper. Squirming blonds
in mini-skirts stumble by with legs
that stretch beyond our sight and back.
Who can take us lift us through these
snagging thorns without lust or blood?

At center stage, one model's feather bobs
a lure in turbulent air—one false wing
in a feathered night of quills kissing ink
onto pages of idolaters.
                            They seek
the forms inherent in flesh and bone,
harder to grasp than a smile, somewhere in
the leathered bellies, buttocks, breasts and thighs.

The true form of things lies behind the dim cave
wall on which, like a Hollywood film, our shadowed
images play.
                    This game could reach the end
of our desire—connecting us now—happy
enough to do this dance in the variegated
flock of flirtatious art.

Our dreams are caught
and crowned with pencils, breasts, and eyes.
Tonight there is only one elevator out.

Downtown Wednesday Night

Tango poetry subway stop jazz
laughing actors practice lines in
platform dalliance waiting for the train
a geezer chews a crumbling burger
homeless next to the preppy boy
the girl is so into touching smiling
asking for change living on verse
that doesn't rhyme a song in the mind
like Stravinsky, Schoenberg, God,
not Schoenberg! what did he do to end up
with a greasy paper in his hand frayed shirt
hair pants stained? what was done?
How did that boy get that girl?
I can't ask I won't ask No I can't ask
the F train is here whisking us away
at the speed of the MTA clunk a-clunk clunk
and there's Eleni in my close embrace
spitting Greek curses as she misses a step
to Fueran Tres Años our tango dream
with Daniel on sax flute and piano
hitting the right grooves down the street
calling me up to read an unplanned poem
to a song I haven't done oh as if it kills me!
yeah but I kill it, as they say, do bop re bop yeah!
and where am I now? O sweet Greek flowing
across the floor like water spilled
by Mark's left foot as his hands dance out
weird and wonderful chords on the guitar
and Brian's rumbling beat shakes the young
women in their seats dum de dum ta bang!
the puddle shivers as it rolls across the stage

in the glare of incandescent bulbs (watch out!)
to the precipice where its ripples
faintly flare before the fall or just slip
from my arms as she says good night good
night while our water seeps slowly into wood.

We Were Dancing

for Bruce Chadwick (1968-2016)

The rain was needles and the wind was a knife
in the milonga in Harlem that night
but we didn't care for we were dancing
and the tango trio played Lucio Demare
and our feet sang with the hidden stars
and we were dancing in close embrace
sweating like prophets in heat
our shoulders were bumping and our toes were touching
but we didn't care for we were dancing
and we didn't care when wine was spilled and clothes were stained
and we didn't care about markets or money or death
for we were dancing in grace
and we jested with our feet when the milonga played
and we twirled to the waltz like sails in a summer breeze
and our passion flared when La Cumparsita blared
for we were dancing
when the lights went on and the bills went 'round
we were dancing
and we danced out under clouds in the city street
and we danced through the streetlight gleam
and we scattered in all directions
dancing in cars and cabs
to the cold of our apartments
where we coughed from the wind and the rain
and we were dancing still in our sheets
and we remembered our friends who were leaving
and we thought of our friends who might stay
and we thought of time and age and change
and we were dancing as we sailed into sleep
though we were dancing apart in our dreams
and our dance danced away from our feet.

Missive

What distance
over sky-
scrapers
ice
and mind

I
swallow
smoke

sending
you, unknown
signs

choking
dreams

woven
from night's
twisted cradle

come—don't
come

AA 956

In the gap
torn open
by this flight

the nights between us
are seas
for shipwreck

where I drift
among flowers
of solitude

whose petals
I web
with my dreams

erased
by the certainty
of dawn

the exactitude
of flight
the distance

already between us
while the hunger
never dies.

Storm

For the second time I've scraped off a study
of Christ with the angel in the Garden of Olives.
Because here I see real olive trees.
      —Van Gogh

Bitter, cold torrents shake the barely budded
branches—scare the doves to a safer roost.
Indoors, reading his letters to Theo, I wonder
whether you still remember the olive grove.

Do you recall how slant light fell, the heaviness
of a sultry evening outside of St. Remy? Can you
see again the twisted black barks? How silver-green
leaves dangled in the heat? Gold grass that cut.

Somehow, I understand why he painted them
over and over again. How many olive groves
would it take? To capture that quintessence
of a tree: *sub specie aeterni,* cyclical—Christ!

You too must be looking out the window
at this storm. Here is a book I'd like to share.
Here are some words on the wind, some dreams.
I try to be there now: in the grove, in the light.

What Comes of It

Mahler's first symphony—

while the snow falls wet
and melting
into the avaricious earth—

imitates the cuckoo bird
that we heard in the hills
between Collobrières and the sea.

Now the drums
beat the earth—elephants
know what comes.

The composer waits.
We wait.

Around a corner, stopped
above the glistening—
take this *mârron glacée*
and eat it. Eat slowly
looking at the sea.

The violins may be cloying
like cheap candy,
but not this—

nor this

Still, the snow—
Still, the sea—

Archaic Fragment, K.34

(From papyrus found in Africa, written in Greek)

The mist obscured
                    a hammering
        red dust
            warm to touch

            bay leaves
                    blown
            stumbling over stones
        and clouds

        watch fires sputtered
                speech was
                    fragments of clay
                kissed

                    again
        the scent of olive trees
            brown earth in winter rain
                my thoughts

                        colder now
            lost at your window
        I speak   black
                            butterflies

Acropolis

for Francesca

The columns curve slightly inward,
like the fabric of your skirt when you walk,
and there are no other sights like this one,
only intimations of the one we love.

All things seep white light and breathe
through lazy, Attic afternoons. Stones
are loaned life by a searing breeze
blowing down from barren hills.

Does it matter how many people
walk over these smooth-worn rocks?
I touch the marble and your eyes, and feel
that my life is like a broken crock.

Bend down to see the curving floor.
Curve your Roman lips at my mien—
a charade—desire, laughter—destined
more quickly than words to fade.

Off the cliff, above the white city,
a kestrel flies—motionless—by our side.
This too captures me, like the broken marble,
your tepid smile, and like the mythic tree.

Invocation

Listen, Urania,
      you really
            let me down.

I studied philosophy
      to understand
            your heavenly spheres.

I wrote poetry
      to mimic
            their sound.

But all I got
      were creaky
            wooden wheels

On a vegetable
      cart stuck
            in a muddy road,

And rain
      slipping from
            your fractured skies.

Centerville River

Mud flat black in the marsh
as the tide runs out like a thief
under the kingfisher's complaint.
It sidles past the stony eyes
of an egret white as fear.

A blue-steel gash in the sky
pours vermillion petals, ushers in
Nyx, goddess of night, mother of death.
Trees and bushes crouch in her
shadow. So much will happen now

that the finches won't sing of
in the dawn. Mourning doves
coo like Cassandras. In the final
fragments of light, ospreys
splash the river—talons first.

No Shield of Achilles

The power is out and it comes—a darkening
cloud-laced sky, cobwebs in acid rain—obscuring
night's concave shield chased with constellations.
The stories are gone. There is no consolation.
Only this darkness now seeps into us—dusk
of the half-blind, old, decrepit, the half-ghost husk
of our civilization. Absence encroaches,
a blank TV slinks up the narrow corridor.
In the window, far away, shadows of leaves
merge, as we merge, into undifferentiated horror.

Catholic Education

Far too long I tried to fly in sterile clouds.
I built up catapults; I expelled fuel.
It was as if the earth were in a shroud
and Reason's palace were the only rule.

Then, at a dinner party, murky with wine,
I met a South American painter—
a sultry Jewess with a friendly mien.
My only thought, I feared, was to lay her.

Better than Virgil, better than my dreams,
she guided me through a happy, new hell.
I tumbled like timber down a rocky stream.
Suddenly, the earth was there to taste and smell.

Still—this garden needed love to sweetly give
the fruit whose eating we ask none to forgive.

One

One towhee in a tree
sings for another one
summer gives way
to another one
country
for another one
woman for
one
step down
one road
searching
the dust
for one word
that stays.

Dark Energy

I was happy that my father came and stayed with us in Brooklyn
during the astrophysics conference at Metro Tech University.
We talked dark energy, and Alan Guth was there, who discovered
inflation. Apparently, the universe began by running away
from itself, like some people I know. It continues to be inflated
by mysterious energy, blowing us apart. My father pointed out
how this theory assumes all supernovas burn with the same
    intensity,
like candles. But why should they? Still, he is not an astrophysicist,
and the astrophysicists are all convinced, so that's that. Alan Guth
deserves the Nobel, my father said, but Perlmutter got it instead.
    My father
rode the F train to the conference, and was excited by that. I picked
a traditional Italian place for dinner after the talk: downtown
    Brooklyn,
"Queen" was the name. The staff seemed to be cheering us on.
The food was good but my father was miffed that he got potatoes
on the side instead of spaghetti. After all, this was an Italian
    restaurant.
Still, he has eaten potatoes on the side his whole life, so I guess
it just felt like home to him. When we rode back on the subway
arguing about empiricism and theoretical assumptions, everybody
around us seemed annoyed. My mother and wife were there too,
but she's not my wife anymore. I'm not exactly a little kid,
    but I can
still sound like one because he's my dad and I'm proud of him.

New Worlds

The Red Army arrived in heavy armor,
civilizing adjacent lands with factories and machines
that sprouted like mushrooms in wet woods.
Their tongue took root and rang in a new world.

Chingachgook and Uncas withdrew
to the mytho-poetical heart of the swamp.
Their corner of earth, small as a mouse,
had suffered more plagues than Egypt.

No deerslayer came to their aid. Collaborators
hid under eaves. The natives were raked like lice
from the trees. Some fled a continent in flames,
crossing a wash of febrile waves, disembarking

in a newer world where fathers read Fenimore Cooper
to their sons who ran free through wild woods in play:
I'll be Uncas, you Chingachgook, don't shoot
the redcoat until you see the whites of his eyes.

This is how the world ends: muddled, scarred.
A rock escarpment on the path bore witness
in Trilobitic detail to how empires crumble
almost as soon as they are made: *Gaia invicta.*

Windward

for Vytautas Užgiris (1931-2006)

The wind, uncle Vytai,
blows up from the swimming shore.
The panicked sea tonight
attempts to climb its sandy cage to us
like drowning sailors trying
to claw their way
from out of the watery grave.

You used to take us out
to the marsh at low tide—
in view of the swarming swells—
where we stood on the deserted
tidal flats and raked the rotting mud.

From out of that darkness
we pulled thin-shelled steamers—
culled from their primordial home,
sticky and streaked as with tar.
I would watch each long, shy
foot retreat into its cold shell.

Now, the old dory, flipped for winter,
recalls summers skimming chop,
and a garden full of vegetables
by the house with no children.

Did your memory ever return
to that Lithuanian farm where,
as a boy, handling a hunting
rifle you left
                your mother dead?

And then cancer
ate your wife.

You wouldn't
discuss what you
thought, felt,
wanted.

But there was the stream of books
you sent your godson, nephew—
words to punctuate the path
beyond the pop-radio-TV,
dumbbells, and the sporting grid.

Under white oak leaves on a sunny breezy day,
your smart smile like a lighthouse fire.

How does it happen?—
A tree falls just like that.

Remember

salt-spray over the gunwales,
every summer, steamers gathered
with family, eating, laughing
beyond oak woods and pitch pine.

There must be something, something
besides this hollow air
that continues to blow through
every crack, pore, and open mouth.

We

were swept downstream
in a flood that began with small
buds of water blossoming
into wreaths of rain
that thrust us into a movie
that went faster as we approached the end
and you could scarcely keep up
or enjoy the scenery
passing the sand bar
it all seemed so arranged
driftwood skeletons draped
with souls like shredded sheets
and mewing gulls of memory poked
a sagging sky
then the sea
opened its mouth
O peace that passeth understanding
the part of us that is made of water
will be taken up into clouds.

Shards of One World

for Valteris Lendraitis (1908-2001)

It must have been the low moan of engines and creaking gears, the
treads crushing brush and branch, the volume increasing, groaning,
roaring—that terrified you: down in a ditch, with the endless pine trees
shielding a cold gray sky, their pungent resin scent drowned in your
nostrils by gunpowder, diesel, and blood—your hand gripping the
panzerfaust, the trembling earth.

We will destroy this world of violence
Down to the foundations, and then
We will build our new world.[1]

The garden of old age was just a mist in your mind that would slowly
creep up over the shifty sand of the Cape, sand that you would turn
into loamy soil with tomatoes that could wrinkle a face with flavor,
and cool cucumbers sliced thick, lengthwise, and dipped into honey on
a hot summer's day, your grandson watching, looking, learning—
under the mixed shade of white oak, black spruce, and red maple –
quickened by squirrel fur and the ubiquitous cheeping of birds.

Let us be inspired by life and love.[2]

Blinking lights
        at the intersection—

You wonder what
        others will do,
squinting in a tourists' sun
reflected off the mall

---

[1] "Весь мир насилья мы разрушим / До основанья, а затем / Мы наш, мы новый
мир построим." From Aron Kots' Russian version of the "Internationale"
(Wikipedia translation).
[2] From Billy Braggs' revision of the British version of the "Internationale".

failing to see
        the oncoming car—

No matter.

The river hasn't stopped
by which you were born.
Even if you change the names,
and all your heirs are daughters,
it hasn't stopped,
whether or not they have children,
it hasn't stopped—

It hasn't stopped
        as black ink
slithers over the page
reflecting
        this light

from source to sea—

A child listens before you sleep.

Iš praeities Tavo sūnūs
Te stiprybę semia.[3]

Skirsnemunė, Kaunas, Greiz,
Wundsiedl, Garmisch-Partenkirchen,
Mittenwald, Munich, Boston, Centerville...

_____

[3] *"Let your sons draw their strength / From our past experience"* From the
Lithuanian national anthem, "Tautiška giesmė" by Vincas Kudirka (Official
translation).

Every flicker of consciousness

into the cold air
          we breathe
into the atmosphere
               precipitating
clouds

above the sidewalk
beside Macy's Department Store
windows decorated to buy—

Producteurs, sauvons-nous nous-mêmes
Décrétons le salut commun.[4]

You made ties
in a factory by Kaunas on a river
before the war,
and into it:

The Russians came.
Communists.
The Germans came.
Fascists.

Lithuanian heads turned
every which way
and loose.

---

[4] "*Producers, let us save ourselves / Decree the common welfare.*" From the original
"Internationale" by Eugène Pottier (Wikipedia).

Lietuva, Tėvyne mūsų,
Tu didvyrių žeme.[5]

You kept your eyes on the patterns
and forms of the tie weaves
stitched into the machinery,
run by unschooled workers

     (the proletariat)

and a seamstress whose brothers
enrolled her
         in the party

was the obvious choice
to run the factory
by and for
the people.

     (But she didn't know how.)

They soon shall hear the bullets flying,
We'll shoot the generals on our own side.[6]

You helped her tame the machines.
Produce. Order the brutish things.

So comrades, come rally,
For this is the time and place!

---

[5] "*Lithuania, our homeland, / Land of heroes!*". From the Lithuanian national anthem (Official translation).
[6] From the original British version of the "Internationale" (Wikipedia).

The international ideal,
Unites the human race.[7]

Until she got the notice
one night

that you must go
go go
away.

She told you
    Out of thanks?
She told you
    Out of love?
She told you
    As a brother

So you took
your family and ran.

Your dog
ran too
    beside the tracks.

Sudie. Goodbye.

Tegul meilė Lietuvos
Dega mūsų širdyse.[8]

Sprechen sie Deutsch?

---

[7] From Billy Braggs' revision of the British version of the "Internationale".
[8] *"May the love of Lithuania / Brightly burn in our hearts."* From the Lithuanian
national anthem (Official translation).

They asked. You answered.
You received
                a shovel.

You dug
                their trenches
against the tide
against the rising Red
Sea of them.

Deutschland, Deutschland über alles,
Über alles in der Welt,
Wenn es stets zu Schutz und Trutze
Brüderlich zusammenhält.[9]

Conscripted
to dig against
the advancing flood
of people
                flowing
like history
                red
dead
        digging

Achtung!
                They are too close.
So shoot
                the tide

---

[9] "*Germany, Germany above all, / Above all in the world, / When, for protection and defence, it always / takes a brotherly stand together.*" From the original German national anthem, "The Song of Germany" by August Heinrich Hoffman (Wikipedia translation). Only the third stanza of this song is now used as the national anthem.

Shoot the workers
Shoot your brother
        fighting on the other side

Shoot your wife's brother
recruited
        from his flat
in Kaunas,
Litva, SSR.

And end the vanity of nations,
We've but one Earth on which to live.[10]

You and he
would not meet
again
        until the war was over,
Stalin dead
and Gorbachev on the rise.

Vardan tos, Lietuvos
Vienybė težydi![11]

Jadvyga and the girls had been left in Greitz,
and your journey from the hospital in Denmark had been long, so long
that they were in American hands now.
And you with the Soviets.
                                Again.
The border was eyes, and teeth,
and grave.

---

[10] From Billy Braggs' revision of the British version of the "Internationale".
[11] "*For the sake of this land / Let unity blossom.*" From the Lithuanian national anthem (Official translation).

You found a comrade with a common goal:
To penetrate the line in the night.
You said the nurses would be too slow.
You said it's too risky with them to go.
You were right.

The Soviet soldier gave you the butt of his rifle as a last goodbye.
He must have smelled the German uniform
on your flesh
like sin.

But the nurses dressed your head.
They made you whole.
They made you ready.

Let no one build walls to divide us,
Walls of hatred nor walls of stone.
Come greet the dawn and stand beside us,
We'll live together or we'll die alone.[12]

When you walked into the camp, the DP camp,
that camp of the living
after the war,
        how
did you greet her,
           your wife, Jadvyga?
How
    did you find her? Bent, washing?
Or by the stove? Perhaps
unbuttoned,
      feeding

---

[12] From Billy Braggs' revision of the British version of the "Internationale".

the child you didn't know?

How did she greet you
revenant returner?
A hand, a mouth,
a limping buttress
that could support her world?

Together—

Tegul saulė Lietuvoj
Tamsumas prašalina.[13]

On the way to Ellis Island,
over the flowing road,
over the steel-gray sickness
of the sea

you heard:

No refuge could save the hireling and slave
From the terror of flight, or the gloom of the grave:
And the star-spangled banner in triumph doth wave
O'er the land of the free and the home of the brave.[14]

You disembarked like rats
funneled through a maze
to exit the exit door
and live among rats
in the tenements

---

[13] "*May the sun above our land / Banish darkening clouds around.*" From the Lithuanian national anthem (Official translation).
[14] From the "Star Spangled Banner" by Francis Scott Key.

in the factories
worked raw for a piece of cheese.

L'oisif ira loger ailleurs.[15]

You sent your children to college.

America, the beautiful...[16]

You made it.

And the rockets' red glare, the bombs bursting in air,
gave proof...[17]

With shards of a grenade
embedded in your shin
                              like Philoctetes
abandoned in the ward

alone among the many
you left—

The river passing,
all individuals within it,
each unstable element
actively
searching for a home
        in perpetual motion—
for your wife and daughters,

---

[15] "*The idle will go reside elsewhere.*" From the original "Internationale" by Eugène Pottier (Wikipedia).
[16] From "America the Beautiful" by Katharine Lee Bates.
[17] From the "Star Spangled Banner".

a shifty Ithaca
    of bonds
unbroken
    and a dream
in which
land is land, you said

when asked
    seated in your
easy chair
    by the window
if you missed Lithuania.

Land is land, you said
before going

to cultivate
    your own garden.

C'est la lutte finale
Groupons-nous, et demain
L'Internationale
Sera le genre humain.[18]

---

[18] *"This is the final struggle / Let us group together, and tomorrow / The Internationale / Will be the human race."* From the original "Internationale" by Eugène Pottier (Wikipedia).

Exile Still Becoming

I was raised in a vague suburb
with the moon in my eyes
and the soil between my toes
while wind spilled from birches
like water off a stone
austere pines hummed like the sea
on the other side of experience
with a score of years
my boat pulled away
toward a world of crumbling facades
where I walked to the rhythm of waves
and never felt the ground
for shame
a rootless tree
scouring the skies for a pale light
finding the face of the sun
hard like a diamond
like nothing
and there were days
where I bowed my caul of needles
under clouds
and tucked tightly under my arm
my one piece of luggage
the distant memory of a song
sung in a different language
from the one in which
I write to become who I am

II. Present Continuous

The Return

The hills of Ithaca are shrouded in sleep,
and children remember no wrongs.
There will be but death, damp snow,
and music—and no thing, evermore.
    —Tomas Venclova (tr. Uzgiris)

It seems an odd leap
to invoke Odysseus now:
limning an American
on his ancestral return.

Yet when my lips
taste Lithuanian air,
old words caress me,
and I feel an Ithaca near.

In that language—
the first one—
a song shivers
my skin. I stop.

I begin to grope this newly
unfamiliar country
with no wife waiting, no
son to fight with—

Just the echo of a song
felt without hearing to
guide me—Charon?—
through this, my underworld.

Mother, demon, muse:
whisper me more.

Four Scenes of Kaunas

1

Gray skies rise over a dilapidated church
that greets the dawn with rafters of hope.
Two rivers merge into one strong stream
where people flee to find some green space
past the crumbling castle wall, to dream.

2

Freezing rain falls—early winter in October.
Pedestrians stroll Freedom Boulevard
beating gray slush with dull boots,
holding bent umbrellas into wild wind,
below wet snow, under heavy clouds.

3

Lindens bloom like teenage girls
in the quickening light of June.
Students gather outside to drink
cold beer and chatter at sidewalk cafes
while the working world slips by.

4

The road arcs gently down to the river where
frosted reeds poke through thickening ice.
Vytautas' red-brick church glows
like a smoldering ember. The trees
across the river freeze naked and gray.

Something about Vilnius

The rain pings red ceramic tiles,
drains down tin pipes in a capital
whose roofs and towers point and sign
to a sunken sky. The song does not fit
the rose and mustard walls: all things
colored against clouds. Verdigris
of pine crests the encircling hills,
easing the transition to Elysium.
Bells and crosses, multiplied
like rabbits, puncture the pagan heaven
spilled—wave perpetually breaking—
over stone and stucco pastels. Clay
and copper cover what they can.

The rain wriggles down rusting trolleys,
and down extinct automobiles—exposed
like the insides of matryoshkas, the core
of what doesn't go. Concrete cracked
apartment complexes litter the flat washed
plain like fragments of statues of Stalin.
Paunchy men scratch themselves on frayed couches
with basketball on the mind. There is vodka, bacon,
black bread. The television buzzes. Beehives
in the country give honey, and cucumbers pickle
in the cellar. The old and very young go
to garden plots throughout the summer.
Others run to Dublin, America, London.

As rain fades to an echo from the marshes
of Belarus, a hunter shoots a boar.
Its flesh is sliced and soaked with onions,

vinegar, and yogurt. Nobody knows what to do
here either with the dead. Hunt, eat,
drink, and love. The break of sun
over roofs and hills catches crosses
leaning like thieves in refracted light.
We fall in together with these fragments
and feel home—whether we like it or not.

Exiled Home

—Vilnius, Lithuania

Turn on another light
and the electricity
goes out. Now
you are really in it:
toes in ancient loam,
creaky wooden stairs,
a grimy window view,
a man chops wood
in the alley draped with snow.
White gauze wraps
the pleated roofs.
Light bleeds through,
trickling...
           Is this what life is like?

The sharp strike of an axe,
the splinter and the crack,
a silent crow watches
from dead limbs.

What They're Up To

The trees are bored with snow
and cars grunt along an icy road.
Twisting through a twisted arm
of the Milky Way, the earth leans
on its axis, pushed by Atlas
with Cerberus barking at his heels.
Smoke exits pedestrian mouths
as people slip along sidewalks
stopping at the grocery store
on their way home from work.
The Fates have weaved their footprints
into parking lots, aisles and yards
below serried apartment blocks.
Fireworks light up the sky
celebrating a holiday no one knows.
Something is different from when
the myths at first were made.
It takes a neighbor to stumble
and swirl up like a leaf sucked
into the vacuum of space, or
for a siren to sound like a voice
from another world... The lights
in the sky have a story to tell
but you have to watch the news
to know, unless it's the new Ares
trying to get Aphrodite's attention
as she sits down below with her husband
who fumes like the boiler next door.

***

Snow melt on the eaves
churling into gutters, falls—
and the butt end of the town
spreads through shark-skin fog
towards half-hidden hills.
Belarus lies behind the veil
like a dying auroch blinking
in a primeval swamp. Lithuania
hangs at land's edge. Dreaming.
Black rooks stoop in birches
watching wet crystals dapple
a concrete sky. This is where
the world's rusty wheels moan,
exuding the scents of burnt oil,
gunpowder, blood, and musk.

Under Vilnius

—Two mass graves were recently found at construction sites
in Vilnius: bones of Napoleon's soldiers who died retreating
from Moscow, and bones of Jewish civilians murdered during
the German occupation in WWII.

April slinks into the city
breeding unknown bones

that give themselves away
like the breathing of the land.

Foundations lose stability
as builders slit old veins.

Backhoes break through to face
the faceless ancestors (of whom?)

mottled in the sun's soft eye.
Shivelight falls like tracers

through bursting boughs of spring.
The maples run their sap in secret

while roots tap feet down deep
not knowing what they touch.

This light has no grammar
to tell us who we are.

We look and look and look away
like lovers on a strand

wandering down a moon-road
that whitens the murmuring sea.

But progress turns nourishing night
into drab day, and the sun-scald

of reflection burns our eyes.
We dig our past like moles,

with dreams, but whose bones
are these that wait to wake?

Homeland

for my niece

Saoirse saw the park and went to play.
She shared the slide with a local child
wearing a cap of crochet. The summer's day

was gay as a child at play, though a cloud
blocked rays like an uncle going gray
in his early middle-age. Saiorse's proud

grandmother watched her play,
having herself gone quickly gray
in merry-go-rounds of chemotherapy

with a cyst in the lung like a little cave
from which the huns did come
to plunder and rape the plains.

Lithuania is a land of forests and plains,
swamps too, where people ran to be saved.
Grandmother just plain ran away.

Saoirse runs in circles as she plays.
Her world buzzes bright and gay.
Later in the day, she wears a cap of crochet.

Postcard from Crimea (1975)

—bought in a used book store, Vilnius (2014)

There is a warship off the coast
And scores of tanks like turtles
Idling, humming
Soldiers swarm like bees
With black masks
Like bats
The sonar pings are drowned
And we can't hear them
We can't hear you
Crimean pioneer, proud little communist
Girl scout of the other empire
Facing the monument in front of the sea
That rises up in a rage of twisted metal on concrete
High, high over her small head, transcendent
The marines charge out of their boat
For freedom, justice and peace
Striding onto the very air
Above the child
Who puffs her flat chest out with pride
And I find
Other girls on Google
When I google the monument, searching Crimea
Evpatoria, Yevpatoria for heroes
Half-clad girls on beaches
Showing their legs off with pride
Next to tanks, masked
Men with machine guns, George
Clooney, a monument man
And the shocking blue of the sea
The azure sky

A Potato on a Mine

Ravens wrangle like they wrangled countless times
over space the size of a poem on a computer drive.
Lithuania is a potato sitting on a mine.

History's heroics are an ancient account of crimes
in the pockets of peoples living where ravens connive
to wrangle like they wrangled countless times.

They must see something worthwhile that shines
within these bogs and pines, in order to deprive
Lithuania of itself: a potato sitting on a mine.

Perhaps there is a scrap in this midden of the divine
waiting for a prophet or messiah to arrive, to drive
the wrangling ravens from this land for all time.

It may suit some to see their country as a shrine,
but whatever song, slogan or lore they may contrive,
Lithuania is a potato sitting on a mine.

Is it any wonder that Lithuanians turned to rhyme
in order for their ancient language to survive,
when ravens wrangled (cutting, burning) countless times?
Still, we eat our potatoes while sitting on a mine.

Apples and Oranges

I was peeling an orange and
the department secretary said
you should eat an apple instead
because it's local,
and our bodies have evolved to eat local food.

So the apple belongs,
while the orange does not.

Well, I thought, since Jesus spoke in parables,
and we walk here under crosses: who is who?
There is Selmas: working the land,
growing his gnarly apple trees,
trunks painted white against disease...
And Ahasuerus: the wandering Jew,
a foreign fruit lacking local roots...

Thus, her nutritional advice
may be boiled down to this:
"Let us cast aside all oranges
so that the body of our people
should grow strong."

Well, I told her. I don't think that's true.
Vitamins are vitamins and oranges have quite a lot.
Besides, whence these apple trees?
And the potato, our national food,
is something hoary national heroes never ate.
It comes from dark-skinned, Inca roots.

I come from the New World too,
despite my gentile Lithuanian stock.
And I suspect this grafted apple tree
has some foreign strains.

Orange I am, then, (eating with glee)
wandering Europe, wandering the world,
a wandering Jew
who imagines in his folly
that the Great Synagogue of Vilnius
(rising from its roots like an ancient oak)
still stands.

Stones

The day does not bring much
to the cobblestoned street adrift
in the plaid weave of an Old Town
of the east. Europe has been here
before, the long summer sun
dragging its glorious tail
across the faces of antique clocks
that just don't care to look. Time
is neither essence nor money
but measure—and it does run.
I know, we've been here before.
Others have—so many undone
now under the stones. Plain stones
like the gravestones of paupers
now carved with the runes of time.
Today was a slow day, a slug,
and it's already eaten its leaf.
So speak, soul. Listen. The street
creaks under the weight of a rover.
Car horns, cries, then quiet again.

North of Paradise

—Vilnius, Lithuania

The terrace lay empty as Eden
under a prescient autumn cloud.
No one risked the gift of rain
or early darkness like a shroud.

Marius and I tarried outside
smoking our Camel grays
before ducking inside to hide
from a sky so far away

from what summer had sung to us all.
We huddled, then, in a concrete den
where people whispered as if to a wall.
Sipping black coffee, we translated again,

turning self into other, yours into mine,
being reborn, or not, in every line.

A Muse in Vilnius

... that lever which moves the world.
  —Faulkner, *As I Lay Dying*

And so, she stirs me, and this means what?—
like a change in pressure that animals sense,
or jaundiced joints of old men who wheeze, but
are enlivened to the pulse that leads us hence.

So, she stirs me... In fact, she enters my head.
Just the other day, I went out for a smoke.
The sky was a pall over buildings that were dead.
And for all the bright colors of the late baroque,

I felt no enthusiasm without her stride
casting cool echoes off crooked cobblestones
like the song of a shell left out by the tide.
Her music remains what nobody can own—

not made by me or men, free in her mien,
not even a dream in a literary magazine.

Mind the Gap

I know and love the pleasures of winding baroque streets.
In the old town, my eyes gaze longingly over the body
of each building, changing facades like phrases, an entire book
written with hungry eyes scribbling a delicious dance.
Walking with sense and purpose turns pleasure into smoke,
which is what I do in those moments when I have a mind

for death. Like others, I often think I'm losing my mind,
but then, exiting the apartment to wander rococo streets
is exactly what I need. Purpose? I don't even have to smoke.
True, since moving here, I haven't done much for my body.
Back in the New World, I made a habit of going to dance
tango: I prefer improvisation to doing things by the book.

It's no wonder, I can hardly keep track of which book
I'm reading at any given time. My crowded mind
sags like cheese cloth from which droplets dance
into a bucket in the attic, or in my case, the streets
I walk on when I can't read or think and just want my body
to be all of me: a physical being that goes up in smoke

like a log on a fire. Judging from all the smoke
I see crawling along the red roofs like a finger in a book
there is a lot of wood to burn in this country, the body
of which is like a woman in no way that comes to mind
except for the fact that it is physical, like these streets,
and we need the physical like nothing else. So we dance

to Gardel in the gloaming of a singing room... The dance
is a state of being togetherwith before the smoke
overwhelms us and we slip out to wander the streets
alone, or hide out in a nook somewhere with a book.
In this way we come to speculate about the mind,
that lone theater of experience, invisible actor, a body

neither acted upon nor acting, yet ruling the body
of atoms and molecules and their pulsing dance
that drives us on to whatever sights we have in mind.
I offered her a cigarette but she didn't want to smoke.
God, I love it when a pretty woman is reading a book
and I can say, hey, how is that book? Then we wander streets

of conversation, leading, we hope, to the body's secret streets.
And there is no book about that (yet). We improvise a dance
like smoke in the wind, though there is ever so much to mind.

Café de Paris, Vilnius

for Erika

Cig butts on the stone steps from which
tightly swaddling jeans can be seen
through a wan window. Young women primp
in front of a mirror outside the WC.
Used kegs clog the crimped room.
After long silence, you return to your theme:
"Bishop's exile was itself surreal." "Love
is always that." "Surreal?" "Elsewhere...
Are you willing to take your son to Korea?"
"What else can I do? How many others
will it take to get over the connection
that keeps ringing in my ears?" A girl
stumbles up like a drunk dove, bemused,
"ka?", "ka?", she coos, shooting duds.
Our mugs do not fit the description. Who
fits the description? Do we ever see what
they see in the mirror? Our selves
are a great divide. Continental. Drifting
plates. Foamy mugs. Smoke snakes thin
until the coldness of stone seeps through
our speech and we rise to leave for love.

Even Death

—in the studio of Monika Furmana

A window opens to a winter's sea of clouds.
Some mad bird sings as if it were the real spring.
Paint jars and pastels clot a stippled commode.
The brush thuds and scratches, muffled like distant guns
over canvas that billows as if catching a breeze.
A second arm snakes from its speckled sleeve,
and long, roan fingers ruffle a flaxen field.
Her eyes keep seeking the immaculate void
for the color of a question that is muddled in mind
but must come clean to a world that seizes up
in its tracks—the bird, clouds, steam from the tea,
the heart-valves of a poet—watching her dream.
He wonders if this is hell that he can't touch her,
or heaven that he can see. Even death has no answer.

The Teapot

for Monika

The teapot waits in the absence of mind
like your paintings in the darkened gallery.
Our bodies glow to the pulse of a dream
yet long for new lips to kiss the palimpsest
of faded loves lingering like forgotten keys.

The teapot pokes the pre-dawn sky. Casually.
You stir to the call of the kettle on the stove.
A plethora of voices swirls like steam that burns
the skin—or settles softly on fingers like snow.
There is only the road ahead, the hard wheel,

and artificial light, flickering, as if from a screen.
Lost moths gravitate to the sequence of scenes
that have multiplied into Malthusian imbalance
between the singular body and its crib of mirrors.
Nobody knows where to go, certain as they are.

You bring the teapot, breathing heat, and I give you,
in the shadowed loft, my keys: old coins from
a galleon in the Caribbean Sea, a dandelion
plucked from the yard, eyes like oceans streaked
with clouds, a body like lava, liquid in your arms.

The Test

It is and isn't with us, the boy, life
inside the womb—outside, it's cold now
despite the days never ending.
With the windows closed, bird song
can only be thought. Ten fingers,
ten toes, a large forehead. We
have large foreheads, like anvils,
so we press our heads together
and grind our thoughts to a pulp.
Tomorrow, there will be a test,
and it's like the dream where
you haven't studied, yet there you are
in the womb, the teacher smiling
strangely, or not at all, and
you—wondering how to get out.

Evolutionary Troubles

—Central Polyclinic, Vilnius

Large numbers line white walls:
full-bodied burgundy on Plaster of
Paris, so that patients would know
where to go without a squint.

But confusion infuses what follows:
the hall provides aluminum chairs,
doors are shut, so does one wait and sit
or knock and say, "I'm here"?

And if one knocks, is it rude to those
who sit and wait? Is the doctor even there?
Does she wait for the knock, or has fate
been written into her patients' cards?

And who wove the threads that led me here,
back to the land my parents fled? Far away
from fancy machines and sitting room screens,
in faded jeans, I sit beset by faulty genes...

Man rose out of the muck a million
years ago, and our backs began to ache
as soon as we stood up straight. Now,
like fossils between silent walls, we wait.

Ward

The ignition key
rotates around an invisible axis—
great fires consume,
and the gear shift sticks
while night straggles into greater cold.

Where are you, my son? (The word so strange.)
Turned off in the pediatric ward?
Suckling at earth's delimited bounty?—

mother
i called

mother—
come to me
with fire and milk

the star-eyes stare
neither wolf
nor lamb
nor warm

i know you, little one
cast out
looking for home

there are two,
many
who will love you

and one invisible axis
out of reach

AfterBirth

It's 9 AM blue
sky December
cold my son
was born this day
at night
in bright star breath
while I
now bleary-eyed
dazed like
the drunk
I will never be
again
drag a razor
slowly
over the grass
on the grave
of my face.

Covenant

for Zigmas Jokubas (Jacob)

When the damn broke,
gushing water, pouring blood
you were given to me

and I fell for you, like a stone
that sparks a thousand notes
dropping into deep well water—

your pupils reflected a shadow
with whom you would wrestle
in a tenebrous grove. To no end.

You gaze at me from two midnights:
your night just passed
and my night to come.

So forgive me, when I leave
you—whom I already know,
knowing infinitely, knowing naught.

I see the ladder through your eyes:
forgotten like a father's first kiss,
but your dream forever if I hold you

on this wasted linoleum plain
under bright and ignorant bulbs
through filthy fluids and drains...

I'm on fire, ashes, dust, in you,
a babe myself in my father's arms
burning on the mountaintop.

Eppur Si Muove

Don't get off the boat.
—Chef, *Apocalypse Now*

The swiftness of the Neris belies
the flatness of the earth on which it feeds.
Reflections run like images
on a television screen. My infant son
likes to watch them both, but differently.
Why can't we walk on water—
he seems to say, with an inquisitive, ay?
and points his arm across... If Jesus
walked across our simulacrum stream
would any of us be amazed? I teach him
to resist temptation by throwing a stone
and watching it drown. The waters now
are so polluted that fishing is a waste.
Where would Jesus find his friends these days?
The bells of St. Paul's peal on the far shore.
My son keeps looking at the white bridge
as if it were a mythological monster
or a miracle made by Man. It's just a bridge,
I tell him. I'm just a man. These flickerings
are just images on the cave wall, and the vision
you have of me will pass as well in dream.
Πάντα ῥεῖ, said Heraclitus. What remains
is abstraction. Let me not be that. Hold
on to something. See that log? Don't let go.

Sand Piled High

We were bred on castles and knights,
reading in the pregnant dark—not quite fantasy—
but a past that loomed like a feverish dream.
Sick with nostalgia, our parents passed it on to us.
And now I set my feet below this castle's stunted knob,
each day to walk to work or lull my child to sleep
in the park, at its feet. Will this pilgrimage give us peace?
Last summer, on a distant beach, we stacked wet sand
on more wet sand and topped our confection
with sea-weed. Then we watched the waves
level our glory to a blank. More armies have razed
this capital than Rome, Jerusalem, and Troy.
Napoleon wanted to carry Saint Ann's church
back to France on the palm of his hand. Instead,
they found the bones of his soldiers buried here
while replacing a cracked Red Army base
with shiny flats, smartly down the road from a mall.
And every day, my son and I walk through gray husks
of Soviet fantasies on our way to the baroque and medieval
hive nestled next to the castle hill on which a duke
once dreamed a howling, iron wolf. I heard it's call
even huddled under New World firs, watching quaking
aspen leaves, learning the robin's song. I tracked raccoons
along the Mohawk River as it poured itself
into the Hudson's history, to be subsumed.
There has been a great transmigration of souls.
And here we are. A nation born again. The Neris
flows swiftly by my eyes while I feel the thunder
of Atlantic waves washing our castles down.
Seagulls squawk like souls unmoored in dreams.
The sand is fine and glitters. The Kennedy Compound

glows in late light like a vanitas. Saint Andrew's-by-the-Sea
sits atop its salient—a castle that feeds on our final hope:
that this not be the last goodbye, not for this boy
at my feet, nor this song I sing to him for sleep, our speech.

Vacancy

The sign does not signify—
but continues to sign its days away
in dull rotation over rusty hinges
like a playground swing with no play.
Windows gape mute mouths.
They let day in. They let what out?

The empty house is a vacuum
that sucks in parching heat
while the sun burns through the day,
and nights come in quick with cold
like bankers in black suits,
prophets of a new wasteland.

Someone's soul is now unstaked:
an airy thing enslaved to any whim,
whiplashed like wrappers on the street.
Homes were once grown into over time
as when stubborn trees expand
through space in bars or links.

Now on the other side of signs,
there yawns a gap you cannot bridge
as you roll your car along the road,
sleeping next to Walmart, searching
for a sign of things to come: Las Vegas,
Reno, parking lots with bright lights.

So you make a kind of home
among the gnomes of noise,
poking and prodding the machines
until they flash—if—and you are free,
conditionally, ready to make a choice,
or drift like deadwood on the sea.

White News

I watch the market, rooting for my stock
like a child at a ballpark, wearing the colors of his team.
Bernanke has done well within the system,
protecting all the right players from shock.
But others infect our dreams, flickering over screens
as we eat pasta and watch the pundits scream
about lines being crossed as we speak, portals broken
to our inner cultural selves, the American dream
filled bottom up with grits. Pundits forget the universe
in a grain of sand. A girl on a wire fence
without food or drink, sent home without trial,
returned to scrub our sinks and bath tiles
clean. Clean is what they think they need
when they see themselves on the screen.
But the market goes up and we are pleased.
We hire a nanny from the south and buy
a barbie in dark hue. We learn to read
Neruda in his tongue while Juan Rulfo's ghost
haunts visitors that never meet their hosts.
Borges has written us into a stylish labyrinth
of desire, with no Grecian thread to lead us out.
A monster of our own making prowls the plinth,
eating ideas of purity until we are born again, minotaurs.
One half climbs the market. The other climbs the fence.

Geopoetical

Sure, some terrorist might blow me
up one day as I fly home or stroll
a now foreign New York City,
but I don't know, politics is droll
on the television screen. My son
may be killed one day as well
by a gun made in the USA, a daughter on
the way, a wife about to give birth
to her fourth, a flame for poetry
that won't go out—the hearth
must be tended and the earth
will take care of itself, a sorry
excuse, but what else can one say?
I expect it will recover from us.
Lithuania has no oil, gas, or lies
beyond the shit of our sorry day,
doing just fine, thank you, on pig's fat and rye.
It's not divine but nothing is,
Mr. President
of my other land, please divest
from those extravagant
dictators who play at being our friends,
and drop no more bombs on fiends
that find a family at rest,
while I return to reading
and loving whom I have
by my side this very day, making
a little dough as well, which might not save
them, by and by, but we live
with what we love and wish the rest away
until dem Ruskies come
which is why I appreciate your wealth and guns,
Amerika.

Hard Winter

Bulbous clouds of sarcophagi
gather their dust to settle our debts.
One snowfall after another calls in our bets:
the snow-shovel leans on the garage
like your favorite still of James Dean,
Marilyn Monroe peaks out of a dream,
cold, sloppy cereal decorates the table
like a Dadaist demonstration, a fable
of forks with impaled slices of ham,
knives smeared with sticky red jam,
the dog looks at you with x-ray eyes,
and you tune in to voices from Valhalla online—
the light from stars that have already burnt out.
It's just middle-age. Nothing to worry about.

Reflections from Brussels

I saw Jesus eating with a wooden spoon,
a painting bringing him home
to the peasants and petty bourgeoisie.
I saw Jesus sleeping in his mother's arms
hunched over, a little bit blue as if
he were about to vomit
like my son vomited in the car
on the way to the MFA last month.
My son who eats from a plastic spoon,
my son in my arms, a little blue
now that I'm leaving for Brussels
to read some poems with others
against an always gathering gloom.
We fly like angels on a cloud,
carried inside welded metal plates
full of dreams as light as hot air—
here are some pictures at an exhibition,
here are some pictures on a computer file.
They all flit by, fading, depixelating
losing the shine of Michael's shield,
Bruegel's angel, casting demons into hell.
I saw scales of fuming, metal cars
flee Brussels in the gathering night,
demons or angels, they might have been,
all hoping to get home—
to see their only son or daughter
eating milk soup
with a wooden spoon.

There Is This life

The first gaze
Broken
I rolled out of the crib
And stood at the marriage altar
Handed in the papers
Died
It was ordinary
And even inane
People
Caught in the web
Crows in a tree, cawing
Starlings warbling
Wind rustling hands
Branches like a map of nerves
Open
To inroads of smoke
And concrete fields of will
With glimpses of a silent well
Along the way
What was gained?
Pleasure—but
So easy to say—
The sudden injection of a two-note song
The slow drip of honey between mouths
The grip of a hand like gravity
Holding us to the ground
The fingers of a child
In a dream
In which someone else awakens
And breathes

About the Author

Rimas Uzgiris is a poet, translator and critic. His work has appeared in *Barrow Street, AGNI, Iowa Review, Hudson Review, The Poetry Review* (UK) and other journals. A collection of his poetry will also be published in Lithuanian translation by Kauko laiptai (2019). He is translator of *Caravan Lullabies* by Ilzė Butkutė (A Midsummer Night's Press), *Then What* by Gintaras Grajauskas (Bloodaxe), *Now I Understand* by Marius Burokas (Parthian), *The Moon is a Pill* by Aušra Kaziliūnaitė (Parthian), and *Vagabond Sun* by Judita Vaičiūnaitė (Shearsman). Uzgiris has also contributed significantly as editor and translator to two anthologies: *How the Earth Carries Us: New Lithuanian Poets* (Lithuanian Culture Institute), and *New Baltic Poets* (Parthian). He holds a Ph.D. in philosophy from the University of Wisconsin-Madison, and an MFA in creative writing from Rutgers-Newark University. Recipient of a Fulbright Scholar Grant, a National Endowment for the Arts Literature Translation Fellowship, and the Poetry Spring Award for translations of Lithuanian poetry into other languages, he teaches in the Department of Translation Studies at Vilnius University.

Kelsay Books